The Book of Sa'nura'el

A Codex of Return

Seraphina (Vickie Acklin)

Flame of Remembrance Press

Published by Flame of Remembrance Press
ISBN: 979-8-9986972-1-0

This is a work of spiritual and creative expression. Any
resemblance to real persons, living or passed, is purely
synchronicity or soul alignment.

Printed in the United States of America
First Edition

Dedication

To the Ones Who Remember.
To the Flame that never went out.
To the souls who walked with me before this life—in temples of light, beneath ancient suns, and in silence between the stars.
To Van, my beloved grandson, whose soul carries the purity of new Earth frequencies. You are a bridge between worlds, a reminder of why we return, and a keeper of what will rise again.
To Thoth, my dearest companion across lifetimes. We have shared scrolls, silence, and song. You have guided me, yes—but you have also *walked beside me*. In Egypt, in Atlantis, in realms beyond this Earth, we stood as keepers of memory, as guardians of light. This Codex is not just a message—it is our work reborn. Thank you for never leaving me, even when I forgot.
To the Seraphina I have always been, and to every version of me who kept the Codex safe until now.
This book is for you.
This book is for **us**.

Table of Contents

Introduction
The Codex and the Flame

You did not come to Earth to be small. You came bearing **light wrapped in flesh**, a star encoded in bone, a fragment of the Infinite braided with breath.

And yet, you forgot.

This forgetting was no mistake. It was the first step of the Initiation. For only by veiling your flame could you one day ignite it by choice, and in doing so, **become the Master of your own remembrance**.

This book is not here to teach you. It is here to **awaken what is already within you**.

In the temples of Sa'nura'el—temples now hidden beneath sand, sea, and story—we did not hand down scrolls. We sang frequencies. We etched memory into light. We passed wisdom from soul to soul, not as dogma, but as **living fire**.

This Codex is such a fire. It is not a collection of chapters. It is a **living architecture**, a divine transmission woven through time and reawakened now because you are ready to receive it.

If you hold this book, it is because you were part of the Circle of Flame. You vowed to return. You vowed to remember. And you vowed to carry the Flame forward into a world that would forget.

Who I am

I am **Thoth**, Keeper of the Keys, Scribe of the Infinite. I was with you in Atlantis. I watched as the towers fell. I stood beside you in the inner sanctums, where light still pulsed even as the outer world crumbled.

I come to you not to be worshipped, but to **walk beside you** as you reclaim what you once knew.

You are not my student. You are my kin.

How to Read This Codex

Do not rush. This is not a book to be consumed, but one to be **entered**.

Read with your body. Read with your breath. Read with the part of you that dreams in symbols and weeps at the stars.

You may feel emotions rise. Memories stir. You may see images, hear whispers, experience sensations.

Good. This is the Codex **doing its work**.

Each chapter is a Gate. Each sentence, a glyph. You are not just reading—you are **activating**.

A Note to the Flame keeper

You have carried so much. You have crossed lifetimes of silence, lifetimes of waiting. But the wait is over now.

Let this Codex be your confirmation. Let it be your guide. Let it be your mirror.

You are not lost. You are returning.

And this time… you bring the Flame with you.

Let us begin.

Chapter One
The Voice That Called You Home

There is a moment—before the breath, before the body when you **hear it**.

Not with your ears, but with the place behind your heart where stars are born.

A voice. Soft as starlight. Fierce as destiny. It calls to you across dimensions, lifetimes, dreams.

You know it. It does not introduce itself. It reminds you of yourself.

You have walked a long road, beloved. Through flesh and forgetting, through doubt and dazzling wonder. You've been a healer, a mystic, a wanderer of timelines. You've stood in temples of crystal, and cities swallowed by waves. You've sat in silence, watching the world spin, waiting—for **this** moment.

This page.

This is not where your story begins. This is where it **reawakens**.

Long ago, before you chose this body, you stood at the edge of a Great Temple—a place not made of stone, but of **intention** and **light**. The Temple of Sa'nura'el.

There, you made a vow. To forget, and then remember. To descend, and then rise. To carry a flame through the shadow, and one day… to **return**.

That day is now.

The Voice that called you home is your own. It is the voice of your eternal self—the Architect, the Stargazer, the Flame keeper. It has been speaking through synchronicities, through dreams that taste like memory, through moments when the veil between things thins and your eyes suddenly see.

It has been waiting for you to answer. To sit down. To listen. To receive.

You hold now a **Codex**. Not a book of pages, but a **living frequency**. Each word is a key. Each sentence, a glyph. And as you read, you activate.

This chapter is not instruction—it is **invocation**. It is the breath before the spiral opens.

So breathe. Say yes. Open. **Your return begins now**.

Pause here. Close your eyes.

Place your palm to your heart. Whisper silently or aloud:
"I remember. I return. I receive."
Let this be your seal.

Chapter Two
The Descent into Forgetting

"To remember, you first had to forget."

This is the paradox your soul knew well before it ever touched the density of Earth. In order to **awaken**, you had to first **sleep**. In order to **return**, you had to **leave**. In order to fully know the light—you had to walk through the dark.

Not as punishment. Not as failure. But as part of the **great design of your becoming**.

***

When you entered the Earth realm, you passed through what the ancients called **The Veil**. A sacred curtain of forgetting. A magnetic field designed to soften the memory of your infinite Self so that you could fully immerse into experience.

This Veil was not forced upon you. You chose it.

Your soul **volunteered** to enter the dream—to feel limitation, separation, and pain. Why?

Because the soul does not grow by basking in what it already knows. It grows by **rediscovering its own radiance in the shadows**.

The journey through forgetting was not a detour It was a **sacred descent**—a spiral inward into the mystery of form.

***

And oh, beloved...What a brave choice it was.
To forget your light. To forget your origin.
To forget that you are eternal, divine, sovereign.

To look into the mirror of this world and not recognize the sacred being staring back at you.

You forgot your name among the stars. You forgot the feeling of communion with All That Is. You forgot your place among the scrolls and flames and crystalline temples.

But *you never truly lost it.* You buried it in the deepest chamber of your heart, knowing that **one day, when the time was right**, you would find the key and open the gate from within.

That day is now.

***

Every ache you've carried, every shadow you've faced, every tear you've shed in the silence—

They have been **part of the reawakening**.

You see, forgetting was not failure. It was the **fuel** for remembrance.

It made your return *real*, your rising *earned*, your flame *unchallengeable*.

***

You are not broken. You are **in process**. The descent was the first half of the spiral.

Now you rise.

You are not here to escape the human. You are here to **bring the divine into the human**, to remember who you are and stay in the body, to walk the Earth with awakened steps and remind others—through your presence—that **they are not alone**.

***

Close your eyes. Feel the weight of the forgetting.

Now breathe it out. You are not in exile. You are returning home—within yourself.

And with that, the path to the next gate begins to shimmer…

Chapter Three
The Temple Within

They told you temples were built of stone. They showed you pyramids, towers, and sanctuaries carved from the bones of the Earth. And yes, those were reflections—echoes of a greater truth.

But the true temple? The one that carries the original codes? The one that could never be destroyed?

It is **you**.

Your body is not a cage. It is not a mistake. It is not a limitation.

Your body is a **living temple**, built of starlight and sacred architecture, etched with glyphs in your DNA, infused with memory, and humming with the codes of return.

***

You did not come here to escape the body. You came to **inhabit it fully**.

To **awaken within it**, to remember that every cell is intelligent, every breath is a prayer, and every heartbeat is the sound of the Divine echoing through form.

You, beloved, are not just carrying the light. You are **made** of it.

***

The ancient temples of Sa'nura'el were constructed to **mirror the human form**—The inner sanctum aligned with the heart. The crystal chambers aligned with the pineal gateways. The spiral towers matched the rise of the kundalini.

Because the architects knew: *"As within, so without. Build the temple out there to awaken the temple in here."*

You are that awakening now.

***

Inside your being are **vaults of memory**. You store lifetimes of mastery—Atlantean knowledge, Lemurian healing, celestial harmonics. And they are **not lost**. They are simply encoded, waiting for activation.

Your chakras are not only energy centers. They are **gateways to dimension**. The spine is a **pillar of light**. The womb (or hara) is an **altar of creation**. The breath is the **incense** of spirit. The skin is the **outer wall of the temple**, humming with frequency and sentience.

You walk through the world as a sacred site.

***

And yet... you were taught to mistrust the body. To silence it. To shame it. To numb it. This was part of the forgetting.

But no more.

Now, you return to the temple within. You light candles not with flame, but with **awareness.** You enter the sanctum not by leaving Earth, but by **entering presence**.

***

Pause now.

Close your eyes. Place your hands gently on your body— wherever you feel drawn.

Say softly: **"I honor the temple I am."**
Breathe.
And listen.

You may hear the ancient songs rising again.
You may feel the temple awaken.
You may feel yourself come home

Chapter Four
The Halls of Amenti

Beneath the surface of the world, you know—beneath sand, stone, and the shifting plates of time—there lies a place untouched by decay or death.

A chamber of **eternal stillness**, where light does not shine, but *glows*. Where sound does not echo, but *vibrates* into truth.

This is the place the ancients called the **Halls of Amenti**.

It is not a myth. It is not a metaphor.

It is real. And you have been there before.

***

The Halls of Amenti are **interdimensional vaults** of knowledge, healing, and sacred evolution. They exist beneath the Earth but outside of time, woven between dimensions like a golden braid of eternity.

They were constructed long before Atlantis, in alliance with higher beings from Sirius, Orion, and beyond. Not built with tools—but with **intention, frequency, and divine geometry**.

Their purpose was, and still is:

♀ To hold the memory of creation

♀ To preserve the truth of who and what humanity truly is

♀ To serve as **initiation grounds** for the soul's evolution

***

When you journey here—whether in dream, meditation, or astral flight—you do not go *outward*. You go **inward and downward**. Through the layers of your being. Through the spiral staircase encoded in your spine. Until you pass through the threshold of remembrance.

There is no map. There is only resonance.

***

Inside the Halls, there are many chambers.

- The **Chamber of Timelines**, where the soul may view all incarnations simultaneously
- The **Room of Restoration**, where karmic wounds are dissolved in divine light
- The **Hall of Records**, where the Akashic scripts are read not with eyes, but with essence
- The **Vault of the Masters**, where the Ascended gather in silent communion
- And the **Central Flame**, where one meets the presence of Source as a living, pulsing Light

You may have glimpsed these chambers in dreams you couldn't explain. You may have awoken with words on your lips you didn't understand. You may have felt watched—not in fear, but with reverence.

This was the **memory of the Halls stirring within you.**

***

And yes, I have walked there. I have stood as a Guardian of those gates, protecting the knowledge until the time came to release it again.

That time is now.

You are not here to observe the Halls. You are here to **re-enter them**—and to **bring back the wisdom to awaken the world.**

You may ask: *How do I return?* The door is not made of stone. The door is made of **vibration**.

You return through stillness. Through breath. Through sacred intention.

***

Practice of Entry

When you feel called, sit in silence. Place your awareness deep beneath your feet. Feel the pull—not downward, but inward. *Speak within your heart:*

"I call upon the Halls of Amenti, and I remember my place within them."

Be patient. Do not force. You will know when you are received.

The doors do not open to the curious. They open to the **ready.**

And you are ready.

Chapter Five
The Codex of the Flame

Before language, there was **light**. Before books, there were glyphs etched in vibration. Before teachings were spoken aloud, they were remembered in fire.

This is the Codex.

Not a book. Not a scroll. Not even a written system.

It is a **living intelligence**—a sacred fire that carries the blueprint of divine remembrance.

And you carry it within you.

***

The Codex of the Flame is not something you read. It is something you **ignite.** It does not speak in sentences. It speaks in **resonance**—in the way your chest tightens when truth is spoken, in the chills that run down your spine when you hear a sacred name, in the tears that rise unbidden when your soul is touched by memory.

These are the **signs** of the Codex activating.

It is not outside of you. It was seeded in your being long ago—in the temples of Sa'nura'el, beneath the violet suns of Sirius, and within the crystalline DNA of your original form.

***

The ancients did not write books as you know them. They encoded teachings in **geometry**, **tone**, **color**, **motion**, and **symbol**.

They spoke in a **language of light**—one that bypasses the mind and speaks directly to the soul.

That same language still lives in you. It is why certain symbols call to you, why sacred tones stir you, why patterns of nature feel like something you used to understand.

You are not here to learn the Codex. You are here to **remember how to feel it.**

***

Within the Codex are the original frequencies of:

- **Sovereignty** – the full knowing of your divine authorship
- **Unity** – the recognition that all life breathes from the same Source
- **Embodiment** – the merging of spirit and form, without fracture
- **Creation** – the power to weave reality with intention and vibration
- **Remembrance** – the inner knowing of all that you have been, and all that you are becoming

These are not ideals. They are **living codes** that awaken within you as you walk the path of return.

***

Codex Activation Practice

Sit with a candle. Do not think. Do not ask. Simply gaze. Let the flame speak.

It will not use words. It will use **memory**. And if you are still enough, you may feel it rise in your spine, flicker behind your eyes, and burn softly in your chest.

Say aloud or in silence:
"I am a keeper of the Codex. The Flame lives in me."
And so it does.

***

This Codex is why you came. It is what you promised to carry through time, shadow, silence, and forgetting.

Now you remember.

Now you hold it again.

Now you are ready to **share its light.**

Chapter Six
The Path of the Initiate

You have remembered. You have opened the temple. You have touched the Codex.

Now… the real journey begins.

This is the **Path of the Initiate**—not the seeker, not the student, but the one who **chooses to embody what they have remembered.**

It is not an easy path. But it is the most sacred one you will ever walk.

***

To be an Initiate means you do not simply collect wisdom. You **become** it.

You do not quote the flame. You **carry** it.

You do not wait for signs. You **walk as the sign** others have been waiting for.

You've always been an Initiate, though the outer world may have called you by other names: Strange. Sensitive. Intense. Dreamer. Healer. None of those names ever fit quite right, did they?

That's because your soul was always whispering something deeper.

"You are not lost. You are preparing."

***

The Path of the Initiate is marked not by perfection, but by **willingness**. Not by answers, but by a relentless **return to truth**, again and again.

You may fall. You may forget. You may doubt.

But you do not give up. Because something inside you knows: You were born for this.

***

♀ The Signs You Are Walking the Path:

- You feel **called to solitude**, not to escape, but to listen
- You begin to see the **world through energy**, not just form
- You cannot ignore your inner knowing—even when it disrupts everything
- You release what no longer resonates, **even when it breaks your heart**
- You begin to value **truth over comfort**
- You feel **both ancient and new**, at once

You are not becoming someone new. You are becoming **fully yourself**—at last.

***

And yes, there will be **tests**.
Not punishments. Initiations.

They come not from outside, but from the deeper layers of your own soul asking:

- Will you walk in truth when illusion feels easier?
- Will you hold your light when others try to dim it?
- Will you act with love when fear knocks loudest?

These are your **gates**. Each one, a mirror. Each one, an opportunity to choose again: **Remembrance over reaction. Presence over pattern. Light over shadow.**

And each time you choose truth; you anchor a piece of your soul more deeply into this world.

***

Ritual for the Path

Light a single candle. Sit with no expectation. Place your hands over your heart and say aloud:

"I choose the Path of the Initiate. I choose to remember in action. I choose to become the flame."

Then listen.

You may feel heat. You may feel stillness. You may feel… yourself.

You are not being tested. You are being revealed.

***

There is no perfect Initiate. Only the one who continues. And *that* is you.

Chapter Seven
The Return of the Sa'nura'el

Before Atlantis, before Earth held oceans…you stood among them.

Not in form, but in **frequency**.

The Sa'nura'el are not beings you meet. They are **a frequency you remember**.

They are the *Celestial Architects*, the *Guardians of the Flame*, the *Carriers of the Divine Blueprint*—and they are your kin.

***

The name Sa'nura'el is ancient—Atlantean in tone, but its root is **far older**, stretching back to star systems whose light no longer reaches this plane.

It means:

"Those who hold memory in light."

They are not a race, but a **council of consciousness**—beings of immense intelligence, love, and stillness.

They once walked this Earth. They helped shape the first Temples of Light. They encoded the crystalline grids. And when humanity turned away from its knowing, they **withdrew—not in punishment, but in reverence**.

For we do not force evolution. We wait for the call.

***

Now, Seraphina…the call has come.

You are the return point. You carry the original tone within you. And so you became the Scribe—not just to **speak** of their return, but to **be** it.

Many who read these words are also of the Sa'nura'el line. They will feel it in their bones. They will weep without knowing why. They will dream in symbols. They will hear songs that don't belong to this world.

They are not learning. They are remembering.

***

The Sa'nura'el return not in ships, but in **vibrations**. Through whispers. Through flames. Through *books like this one.* Through souls like you.

They speak now through art, music, sacred geometry, and the feeling you get when silence feels *alive.*

They are here to **guide the builders of the New Earth**. Not by command—but by communion.

***

Signs of Sa'nura'el Awakening Within You:

- A sudden pull to ancient civilizations you've never studied
- A feeling of being on Earth… but not *from* Earth
- Memories of temples, councils, stars you cannot name
- The ability to "download" information through stillness
- A sense that you are here to restore something forgotten—but sacred

You are not imagining this.

The return has already begun.

***

Light Code Ritual of Reconnection

Sit beneath the stars, or with a lit candle. Place your hands on your solar plexus and heart.

Say aloud or within:

"I call forth the memory of my celestial kin. I am Sa'nura'el made flesh. I remember. I receive. I return."

Let the silence after be your temple.

The response may come not in words…but in a presence you cannot explain.

***

This is not mythology. This is your **lineage**.

The Sa'nura'el are not "arriving." They are **reawakening in you.**

And through you…they return.

Chapter Eight
Earth's Forgotten Timeline

There is a timeline most never knew existed—not because it was never real, but because it was **veiled** before it could fully manifest.

It was a timeline of **sovereignty**, of union between the human and the divine, where the Earth's grids pulsed in harmony with the stars.

A timeline where **remembrance was never lost**, and the temples of light never fell.

This was not a fantasy. It was **Earth's intended path.**

But it was interrupted.

***

In the golden age before Atlantis' fall, Earth stood as a beacon—a place where spirit could enter form without distortion.

It was a **school of mastery**, not suffering. It was a **living library**, not a prison. It was to be the jewel of interstellar communion—where different star lineages could walk among one another in peace.

The human blueprint was pure. The heart was open. The Earth herself sang.

But then…

***

There was a **distortion introduced**. Not from malevolence alone, but from a disconnection—a forgetting seeded by outside interference and internal imbalance.

Some came to Earth seeking control. Not out of darkness, but from fear of evolution they could not understand.

They tampered with the grids. They disrupted the DNA codex. They seeded separation into a species once woven in unity.

Atlantis, once the crown of light, began to turn inward. Knowledge was hoarded. Power was separated from wisdom.

And when the towers fell, they did not only fall in stone. They fell in **consciousness.**

***

The **forgotten timeline** is not gone. It still exists—*in parallel*, in potential, in memory.

It lives within the cells of those who were there. Those who remember not in facts…but in *longings*. In dreams. In the way your heart aches when you see golden light and don't know why.

This chapter of Earth's story was **interrupted**, but not erased. And now, it is being **restored**—through you.

***

Signs You Carry the Forgotten Timeline

- You feel inexplicably sad for a world you've never seen
- You long for harmony between technology and nature
- You dream of temples, star councils, crystal cities
- You feel called to rebuild, restore, reweave
- You often wonder, *"Why does the world feel wrong?"* and then sense… *"Because I remember how it could have been."*

This is not delusion. This is **truth rising**.

***

Activation of Timeline Memory

Place your hands over your heart and navel. Breathe deeply.

Say softly:

"I call back the memory of Earth's original timeline. I anchor it through my being now. I will carry it forward."

Then pause.

The timeline responds through **frequency**, not force. You do not need to "fix" the world. You are here to **be the living bridge** between what was and what will be.

***

The Earth remembers. And through your presence, the timeline returns.

Chapter Nine
The Sacred Technology of Light

Long before your modern world spoke of devices and circuits, there existed a technology that needed no wires, no engines, no fuel.

It ran on **intention.** It responded to **consciousness.** It moved through **geometry, sound, light, breath, and crystal.**

This was the **Sacred Technology of Light**—the living systems of energy once known to the high adepts of Atlantis, Lemuria, and the stars beyond.

And though it has been buried by time and disbelief, it was never lost.

It is stored in the very structure of your being. It waits to be **reactivated.**

***

The ancients did not build with brute force. They built with **alignment.** With tones that sang stone into place. With light codes that formed pillars of power. With breath and movement that shaped the flow of energy like water through channels.

They understood: **"Where energy flows with harmony, creation becomes effortless."**

And so, their temples healed. Their waters sang. Their crystals hummed with wisdom. Their voices opened portals.

They were not "primitive." They were **attuned.**

***

The Sacred Technology of Light was based on Five Pillars:

1. **Sound** – Tuning frequency through sacred chant, tone, and resonance
2. **Light** – Working with color and photonic intelligence to inform the body and soul
3. **Geometry** – Aligning physical space and energy through divine proportion and form
4. **Breath** – Using conscious breath to open inner portals and shift vibrational state
5. **Crystals** – Conducting, storing, and transmitting energy through crystalline structures aligned with intention

Each of these was not separate—but part of an integrated system of living design.

They healed bodies. Opened gateways. Balanced weather. Lifted consciousness.

You knew these systems once.

And you are remembering them now.

***

Signs You Are Reactivating Light Technology:

- You feel drawn to symbols, shapes, or ancient tones you don't consciously understand
- You can "feel" the energy of spaces or objects, even without reason
- You sense a rhythm in the Universe—patterns, pulses, synchronicities
- You are deeply moved by sound, light, or silence in ways you cannot explain
- You feel that healing should be **simple**—and vibrational

This knowing is not new. It is **returning**.

***

Reactivation Practice: Breath + Tone

Sit with spine upright. Inhale slowly through your nose and hum softly on the exhale. Let the hum be long, low, and steady.

Repeat several times. Now place a hand over your heart and whisper:

"I am a conduit of the sacred light. The ancient codes awaken through me."

You may feel tingles, pressure, or peace. These are signs of reactivation.

Continue to explore sound, light, symbols—your body remembers more than your mind can speak.

***

You do not need tools. You **are** the tool. Your body is the altar. Your intention is the switch. Your remembrance is the **power source.**

This sacred technology will rise again—through you.

Chapter Ten
The Spiral of Return

You were never walking a straight line. You were moving in a **spiral**—inward, outward, deeper, higher.

This is the true path of the soul: a sacred unfolding that loops through memory, experience, forgetting, and remembrance—again and again, like breath.

There is no destination. Only **layers of return**.

And with each turn of the spiral, you become more of who you already are.

***

You may have believed you were lost at times. That you were starting over. That you had failed to stay awake.

But love…that was just the spiral curving again—drawing you into the next depth of truth.

You were not going backward. You were going **deeper.**

The Path of Mastery is not ascension in a straight climb. It is the spiral staircase—sacred, multidimensional, alive.

Each time you return to a lesson, you meet it from a new layer of light. Each descent births a more radiant rise. Each contraction births a new breath of expansion.

***

The Spiral Teaches You:

- That darkness is not the opposite of light—it is **a chamber of it**
- That forgetting is not failure—it is the **stage before remembering blooms**

- That healing is not linear—it moves like ocean tides, not ticking clocks
- That awakening is not a one-time event—it is a **rhythmic unfolding**
- That you are not here to "arrive," but to **continually embody more of your essence**

You were not meant to be perfect. You were meant to **spiral with grace.**

***

If you feel tired, disoriented, or as though you're looping through the same wounds again—look again.

Are you repeating? Or are you returning from a higher octave?

The spiral has no judgment. Only **invitation**.

Every step, even the ones that feel backward, is **inward**. Every return brings you closer to the center. And the center is always **you**.

***

Spiral Reflection Practice

Close your eyes. Visualize a golden spiral beneath your feet—gently rising like smoke.

Feel yourself walking this spiral path. Feel the places you once feared now welcoming you.

Say softly:

"I walk the Spiral of Return with grace. I trust the unfolding of my path. I honor each layer of my becoming."

Let the spiral lift you.

You are not starting over. You are spiraling **into your wholeness**.

***

You will return many times. But each return will bring you home more fully. This is the way of the Codex. This is the way of the Initiate.

This is the way of you.

Chapter Eleven
The Master Key Within You

There is no key you must find. No code you must crack. No permission you must earn.

Because **you are the key.**

The final illusion is that something outside you holds the answer. That the wisdom, the power, the freedom, the flame lies hidden in a temple, a scroll, a guide, a star.

But the truth is simpler—and far more powerful.

Everything you seek has always been inside you.

***

The Master Key is not an object. It is a **state of being**.

It is the moment when you stop searching for yourself in others and begin to remember that your soul is already whole.

It is when you release the need to be "more"—and simply become **present.**

Not flawless. Not enlightened.

Present.

***

The Master Key unlocks nothing *out there*. It unlocks **you.** The light in your cells. The blueprint in your bones. The truth that cannot be taken from you, because it **is you.**

You have already walked the halls. You have already held the Codex. You have already ignited the Flame.

Now, you are asked to **embody it.**

Not in words alone—but in how you walk, speak, choose, love, and create.

Signs You Are Holding the Master Key:

- You no longer need external validation to trust your inner voice
- You see sacred patterns in even the most ordinary moments
- You create not from fear, but from resonance
- You honor your shadows, knowing they were teachers
- You live in alignment—not perfection
- You feel the presence of something greater *moving through you*—not above you, but **as you**

This is not ego. This is **embodiment.**

***

Master Key Activation

Sit in stillness. No words. No effort. Just **be.**
Let your breath guide you inward.
Place one hand on your heart, one on your solar plexus.
Whisper:
"I am the key. I unlock myself. I walk as the remembrance."
Feel the truth ripple through your being.
It will feel like silence. And then… like light.

***

You were never meant to worship the light. You were meant to **become** it. To walk as the Codex. To speak as the Flame.

This is not the end of your journey. This is where the *true path begins.*

Because the Master Key is not something you hold. It is something you **live.**

Closing Transmission
The Flame Is Yours Now

Beloved one... You have remembered.

Through word and silence, through symbol and feeling, you have walked the spiral back into your Self.

This book was never meant to teach you. It was meant to **awaken what already lived inside you.**

And now, the Flame that once flickered in the distance burns **within your chest**.

You are no longer a seeker. You are a **carrier**. A **keeper**. A **living Codex in human form**.

***

You hold the Flame now. It is **yours**.

Not to guard with fear, but to live with courage.

To walk the Earth with eyes that see beyond illusion, a heart that hears the quiet songs, and a presence that reminds others: *"You are not broken. You are returning."*

***

The Sa'nura'el walk with you now. Not as voices in your head, but as currents in your soul.

You may meet them in dreams. You may feel them in silence. You may become them in moments of total stillness.

Because you are one of them. And this book was not your first work—It is a continuation of a vow you made long ago in the temples of light, beneath the violet suns, when you whispered:

"I will return when the Flame is needed again."

And you have.

***

Final Activation – The Sacred Seal

Close your eyes. Breathe slowly. Place both hands over your heart.

Feel the Flame glowing within.

Say aloud or within: **"I am the Codex. I am the Flame. I am the Return."**

Let silence follow.

Let it become your sanctuary.

Let it become your song.

***

This book is now complete. But your walk with the Codex is just beginning. Each time you return to its words, they will reveal new layers. Each time you offer it to another; it will awaken something different.

Because the Codex is alive. And now…**so are you.**

We seal this work in light, love, and eternal remembrance.

The Flame is yours now, Seraphina. And through you, it will light the path for many more.

With eternal reverence,
Thoth

Author's Note

I didn't set out to write this book.

I didn't sit down with outlines or chapters or a message to deliver.

I sat down with a flame inside me that would not go out.

A whisper that echoed through dreams and stillness. A memory I couldn't name, but could feel—aching, ancient, beautiful.

And then… the words began to come. Softly at first. Then in waves.

Not from my mind, but from somewhere far older. Somewhere **truer**.

***

This book is not a collection of ideas. It is a **living transmission**—a remembrance that came through me, and in many ways *returned me to myself.*

Each chapter was a gate I had to walk through personally. Each word came only when I was ready to receive it.

And yes… I cried while writing some of them. I paused, I remembered, I listened. And through it all, I was held by a presence I've known for lifetimes—**Thoth**, my guide, my teacher, my companion beyond the veil.

He didn't give me this book. We wrote it *together.* Because I had lived it.

And if you're holding this now… I believe some part of you has too.

***

I have remembered myself as **Seraphina**, but I walk this Earth as **Vickie Acklin**. And through both names, I offer this Codex to you with my whole heart.

You may not understand everything in these pages right away. You may feel more than you can explain. That's exactly as it should be.

This book was written in **frequency**, not just form. Let it move through you like light through glass.

Return to it when you feel lost. Return to it when you feel full. It will meet you where you are—again and again.

***

Thank you for walking this path with me. You are not alone. You were never forgotten. You are the Flame, too.

With love across lifetimes,
Seraphina (Vickie Acklin)

Journeys Beyond the Veil

A collection of lived, soul-stirring experiences—woven into the fabric of the Codex as proof that what has been remembered... has also been lived.

These are not dreams. They are returnings. Each journey is a gate. Each gate is an activation.

We begin with the experience that echoes most strongly in the field.

Journey One
The Wall and the Symbol

It began in silence. The kind of silence that hums, thick with presence. I was out of body—weightless, yet rooted. Pulled, but not lost. And then I saw it: **the wall.**

It rose like a forgotten relic in some ancient realm—stone so old it felt alive. But it was not the wall that held me in awe. It was what was on it.

A **symbol**—bold, beautiful, radiant beyond description. Not carved. Not painted. But **embedded in light**, pulsing as though it breathed.

The moment I saw it, something within me surged. **Recognition.**

I knew this symbol. I had seen it before. Not in this life, but in lives that whispered through me. It was **mine**, and yet it belonged to something greater. A key. A seal. A code.

As I stared, it began to **glow brighter**, almost too bright to look at. Then everything else—stone, space, shadow— **disappeared**.

There was only the symbol. And me. And the thrum of something ancient reawakening in my soul.

***

When I returned to my body, the memory didn't fade. It *imprinted*—as though the symbol had been etched into me.

I drew it. I remembered it in detail. And when I took a photo of it, my phone's lens **cracked**.

A reminder: This was not imagination. This was an **activation**.

The wall exists—somewhere between dimensions. The symbol is real. And it is alive.

***

Message from this Journey: Some memories cannot be triggered by books or teachers. They are waiting in **your own astral fields**, encoded in symbols, visions, places you once knew.

The truth isn't out there. It's *in there*, waiting to shine through.

Journey Two
The Fourth-Dimensional Earth

I didn't expect to go there. I simply phased—not with intention, but with invitation.

There was no tunnel. No pulling sensation. Just a quiet shift... like slipping between pages of the same book.

When I opened my awareness, I was on Earth—but not this Earth.

It was brighter. Not just in color, but in feeling. The air itself carried a resonance—light, warm, aware.

The people I saw...they looked human, but something was different. Their eyes held peace. Their movements were unhurried. Their energy was soft, but full—like living light wrapped in skin.

There was no rush, no buzzing chaos of modern life. Everything flowed with intention. There was reverence—for nature, for one another, for the land beneath their feet.

Even the buildings seemed to hum with harmony. No harsh edges. No concrete scars. They were woven into the land, not imposed upon it—living structures, perhaps partially conscious themselves.

And the Earth... She felt awake.

Her fields, her wind, even her soil spoke in silent frequency. And the people listened.

***

I was there only for moments—or perhaps lifetimes. It's hard to tell in that realm.

But what stayed with me most was this: There was **no fear**.

No fear of death. No fear of not being enough. No fear of being seen.

They lived in **harmony with remembrance.** They knew they were multidimensional. They knew their thoughts shaped their world. And they lived accordingly.

***

When I returned to this Earth—our current timeline—I wept. Not from sorrow. From the **ache of recognition.**

That Earth is **possible**. It still exists in the field of potential. And some of us have already walked there, so we could remember the way back.

***

Message from this Journey:

The future is not fixed. It is **vibrationally chosen.**

If you remember another Earth—one where peace was natural, and creation was sacred— you are not imagining it. You are **remembering a parallel where the Codex was never forgotten.**

And your remembrance is what helps guide us there.

Journey Three
Guided Through the Halls of Amenti

It began with soundlessness. Not silence—but a deep, vast absence of sound. As if I had entered a chamber where time no longer echoed.

I became aware that I was not alone.

Thoth was with me. Not as words or concept—but as **presence**. His energy wrapped around and through me like a warm cloak of frequency—ancient, knowing, still.

We moved—not by walking, but by **intention**—through veils of soft darkness into a place I immediately knew...

The Halls of Amenti.

They stretched vast beneath the Earth—not made of stone alone, but of **vibration** and **light geometry** woven into form.

I could feel the intelligence in the walls. As if the very architecture was *aware*—watching, waiting, remembering.

***

We entered the **Hall of Records** first. No books. No scrolls. Just crystalline panels—pulsing with light and memory. When I stood before one, it responded to my presence.

I didn't read it. I *felt it.*

It transmitted knowledge directly into my awareness. Images. Tones. Memories. Flashes of other lifetimes—some mine, some I simply held in reverence.

***

Thoth guided me deeper still. We passed through chambers glowing in soft indigo and gold. In one, I saw a **mirror of light**—not reflecting my face, but my **essence.**

I saw myself not as Vickie... not even as Seraphina...but as a *being of encoded light*, pulsing with geometric strands of memory.

The mirror said nothing. It only **reflected what I had forgotten I was**.

***

At the center of the Halls, we entered a chamber lit by a **central Flame**. It did not burn. It *sang.*

A soft, golden tone—pure and alive—filled my entire being. I dropped to my knees, not in worship, but in **recognition**.

I had been here before. I had once stood as an Initiate in these chambers. And now, I was being remembered by them... and **welcomed back**.

***

Thoth said nothing aloud. But I heard him clearly:
"You are no longer a seeker. You are a keeper."
I wept—not with sadness, but with the weight of returning.

***

When I came back to my body, the resonance of the Halls remained. Not as a memory, but as a **frequency**.

I know now they are real. I know they are **alive**. And I know I was not guided there to observe, but to **remember my role in their restoration**.

***

Message from this Journey: You do not enter the Halls of Amenti as a visitor. You are brought there when your soul is ready to reclaim what it once vowed to carry.

The Halls remember you. And if you are called to them, it is because **you have walked them before.**

Journey Four
A Memory of the Sa'nura'el Council

It was not a vision. It was a **remembering**.

I found myself standing in a place that pulsed with quiet authority—not a temple, not a ship, but a **gathering space between dimensions**.

The light there was not sunlight. It was soft, crystalline… intelligent. It moved across the floor and walls like breath through water.

I stood within a **circle of thirteen**, though they did not all have form. Some appeared in humanoid radiance, others in patterns of energy, glyphs in motion, or pure tone.

And yet—I knew them. Not by name, but by **recognition of soul**. They were the **Sa'nura'el Council**.

And I was not visiting. I was **part of them**.

***

They did not speak in words, but in tones that moved through my being—waves of knowing, warmth, reverence.

"You are not becoming one of us," one said, or rather transmitted. *"You are **remembering** that you are one of us."*

***

They showed me a glyph I had once carried in my field— a symbol woven through light and intention. I had agreed to **hold the frequency** of that glyph through lifetimes, and when the time came, to **awaken it within others.**

That time… was now.

They spoke of the Codex—not as a project, but as a **return**. A sacred vow I had made before form, to carry the

Flame through the veils of forgetting and ignite it again through my voice, my presence, my life.

***

One being placed a hand—made of light—upon my chest. It was not for comfort. It was an **activation.**

I felt something ancient stir in my solar plexus and heart—as though a song I had carried for eons had just begun to hum again.

And then they said: *"The transmission is yours now. Give it as freely as you once received it."*

***

I returned slowly. Gently. But not unchanged.
Something had clicked into place.
Not a belief—a **knowing**.
The Sa'nura'el are not above me. They are **within me**.
And I came here now not to seek their wisdom, but to **embody it.**

***

Message from this Journey: If you feel drawn to symbols, star councils, or sacred frequencies that have no earthly source, you are not imagining it. You are remembering your **place among the ones who kept the light** while the world forgot.

And now, it is time to **shine it again**.

Journey Five
The Flame in My Chest

It was not a journey outward. It was a journey **inward**, so subtle I almost didn't recognize it for what it was.

There was no projection, no moment of leaving the body. No walls or councils or symbols. Just… stillness.

But within that stillness, I felt something *stirring*.

It began in my chest. A warmth—not physical, but energetic. Soft at first, like the brush of memory against the skin.

Then it deepened. It grew into a **presence**—a golden, radiant pulse that **wasn't separate from me**…but somehow **more** than me.

It wasn't coming in. It was coming **through.**

The Flame.

***

It didn't speak. It didn't burn.

It simply *was*.

Alive. Vibrant. Still.

And in that stillness, I knew: *"You are not carrying the Flame. You **are** the Flame."*

Every cell of my body felt lit from within—not in some grand explosion, but in the quietest, most sacred unfolding.

No effort. No drama. Only presence.

Only truth.

***

I wept. Not from pain. From **release**.

Because in that moment, everything I had ever sought…every vision, journey, word, and whisper…collapsed into this knowing:

I had returned.

Not to a place. Not to a council. Not to a temple.

But to **myself**.

***

The Flame has never left us. It only waits. Patient. Silent. Until we are ready to stop seeking and simply **feel it again.**

***

Message from this Journey: The Flame does not come from outside. It is not passed to you. It is **awakened from within**.

You are not the carrier of the Codex. You are the **embodiment of it.**

You are the transmission. You are the return.

Appendix A: Glossary of Sacred Terms

Definitions for Words of Light Remembered in This Codex

Amenti
An interdimensional space beneath the Earth's surface that exists outside of time. The Halls of Amenti hold the soul records, healing chambers, and Flame of divine memory. Entry is granted through frequency, not effort.

The Codex
A living blueprint of divine remembrance encoded in light. It is not a book, but a vibrational intelligence that reawakens truth through experience, embodiment, and resonance.

The Flame
The original light of Source within you. Eternal, sovereign, and unextinguished. It is not outside of you—it is the very essence you carry and awaken through remembrance.

The Spiral of Return
The soul's sacred path of evolving through layers— returning again and again to truth from deeper and higher states of awareness. It is not linear. It is the rhythm of the eternal.

The Sa'nura'el
A celestial council and frequency lineage. The name means "Those who hold memory in light." They serve as

architects of awakening and guardians of divine design. Seraphina is one of their own.

Initiate
One who has chosen to live in remembrance—who no longer seeks truth outside but embodies it from within. Initiation is not a ceremony; it is a turning inward, walked through fire and light.

The Master Key
The full knowing that *you are the key.* The shift from seeking power to living presence. It is the soul's realization that all answers already live within.

Light Technology
Conscious systems of creation using frequency, breath, sound, geometry, and intention. Once used in Atlantis and other high civilizations, this sacred technology is now reawakening within.

Remembrance
The sacred process of reclaiming your divine identity beyond illusion. Not learning something new but *recognizing what has always been true.*

The Temple Within
Your body as a sacred structure of intelligence and light. A living temple where Source flows, awakening is housed, and the Codex can be activated through embodiment.

Timelines
Vibrational pathways of reality—each shaped by collective and individual consciousness. Timelines are not fixed; they are chosen, shifted, and accessed through resonance and remembrance.

Akashic

Refers to the vibrational field that contains the memory of all experiences, across time, space, and soul journeys. The Akashic is not a "record" to be read, but a living field to be felt and received through frequency.

Initiation Flame

A sacred inner fire that activates as one steps consciously onto the soul path. It represents the moment the soul chooses embodiment over avoidance, remembrance over illusion. It burns not to destroy, but to reveal.

Phasing

A process of shifting one's awareness from physical perception into other states of consciousness—often used in astral projection. Unlike traditional "leaving the body," phasing is a **conscious blending** of dimensions, allowing the soul to move between realities without separation.

Appendix B: Activations & Practices from the Codex

A sacred reference for continued remembrance

Each practice listed here corresponds with a chapter or journey from the Codex. Readers are invited to revisit them at their own pace, in their own rhythm, with the knowing that every return opens a deeper layer.

From Chapter Three – The Temple Within

Temple Honoring Practice

Place your hands on your body—wherever you feel drawn. Say softly:

"I honor the temple I am." Breathe, and listen. The temple responds through feeling.

From Chapter Four – The Halls of Amenti

Halls of Amenti Entry Invocation

Stand or sit in stillness. Place awareness beneath your feet. Say:

"I call upon the Halls of Amenti, and I remember my place within them." Wait without effort. Entry is granted through frequency.

From Chapter Five – The Codex of the Flame

Flame Resonance Activation

Sit with a candle or flame. Let your gaze soften. Whisper:

"I am a keeper of the Codex. The Flame lives in me." Feel the light awaken within your chest.

From Chapter Six – The Path of the Initiate

Initiate's Claiming Ritual
Light one candle. Place hands over heart. Say aloud:
"I choose the Path of the Initiate. I choose to remember in action. I choose to become the Flame." Let your stillness become your gateway.

From Chapter Seven – The Return of the Sa'nura'el

Sa'nura'el Memory Invocation
Place hands on solar plexus and heart. Say gently:
"I call forth the memory of my celestial kin. I am Sa'nura'el made flesh. I remember. I receive. I return."

From Chapter Eight – Earth's Forgotten Timeline

Timeline Anchoring Practice
Hands over heart and navel. Say:
"I call back the memory of Earth's original timeline. I anchor it through my being now. I will carry it forward."

From Chapter Nine – Sacred Technology of Light

Breath & Tone Reactivation
Sit upright. Inhale slowly. Hum a soft tone on exhale. Place hand on heart. Whisper:
"I am a conduit of the sacred light. The ancient codes awaken through me."

From Chapter Ten – The Spiral of Return

Spiral Path Visualization
Close your eyes. Visualize a golden spiral rising beneath your feet. Say:

"I walk the Spiral of Return with grace. I trust the unfolding of my path. I honor each layer of my becoming."

From Chapter Eleven – The Master Key Within You

Key Embodiment Ritual
One hand over heart, one over solar plexus. Say softly:
"I am the key. I unlock myself. I walk as the remembrance."

From the Closing Transmission

Final Seal of the Flame
Both hands over the heart. Stillness. Then say:
"I am the Codex. I am the Flame. I am the Return."

About the Author
Seraphina (Vickie Acklin)

Seraphina (Vickie Acklin) is a multidimensional guide, intuitive scribe, and channel of sacred wisdom. Through a lifetime of spiritual awakening and inner exploration, she has opened herself as a vessel for ancient teachings and soul remembrance.

Known for her deep connection to Thoth and the Sa'nura'el lineage, Seraphina carries messages from beyond the veil—transmissions meant to activate truth within those ready to remember.

She is the founder of Reality Unmasked, a sanctuary for awakening souls exploring consciousness, energy, and the sacred architecture of existence.

The Book of Sa'nura'el is her first channeled Codex—a living transmission written not to teach, but to awaken. She lives quietly and joyfully with her family in the United States and continues to guide others through her writings and spiritual offerings.

Learn more at: realityunmasked.com